MAKING MONEY WHILE YOU'RE SLEEPING

MY JOURNEY AS A KID ENTREPRENEUR

Written By: Sean Gilmore

Illustrated By: Russell (Trio) Gallien, III

To my mom, Vanessa Gilmore. Thank you for your love, support and encouragement.

Love,

Sean

MAKING MONEY WHILE YOU'RE SLEEPING

MY JOURNEY AS A KID ENTREPRENEUR

I'm Sean Gilmore, and I just completed the eighth grade at the River Oaks Baptist School in Houston, Texas. I play football in the fall and I play lacrosse in the spring. On the weekends, my friends and I enjoy playing Xbox together.

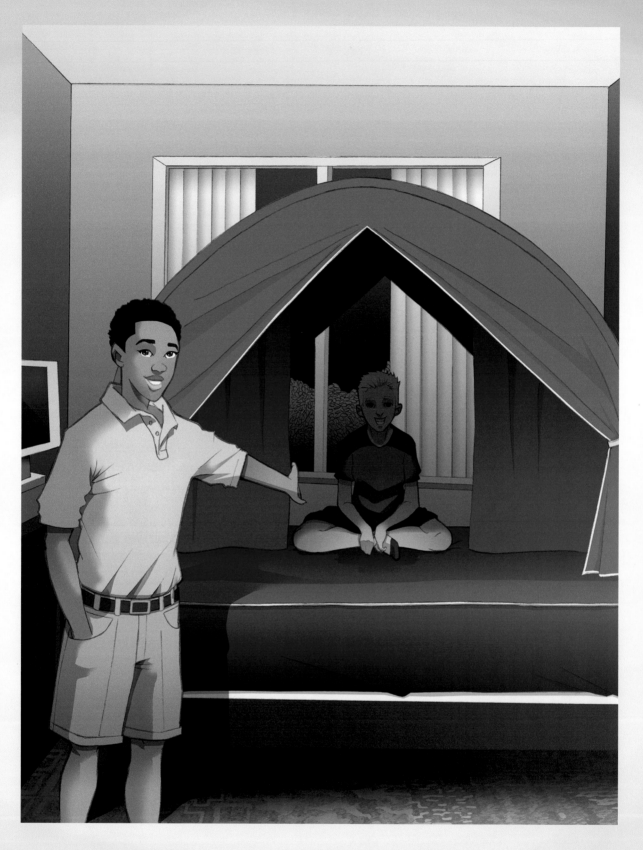

I'm just a regular kid, except that when I was thirteen years old, I became the owner of the Sleepover Bed Tent Company, home of the "Slumber Separator", the unique solution for sleeping single in a double.

My journey as a kid entrepreneur began when I was ten years old, in the fifth grade at River Oaks Elementary School. That year, I entered the Inventor's Showcase at my school. My teacher encouraged us to think of new solutions for everyday problems.

I liked having my friends over to spend the night at my house. I thought about how much we liked building forts. Because I only had one bed in my room, I also thought about how much fun it would be to build a tent where you could hang out when you wanted to enjoy your friend's company, and then have your own private sleeping space when it was time to go to sleep.

I built a model of a bed tent and entered it into the Inventor's Showcase. I won second place at my school, so I was able to display my invention at the Children's Museum of Houston. So many kids liked my invention that I asked my mom if she would help me make it into a real product.

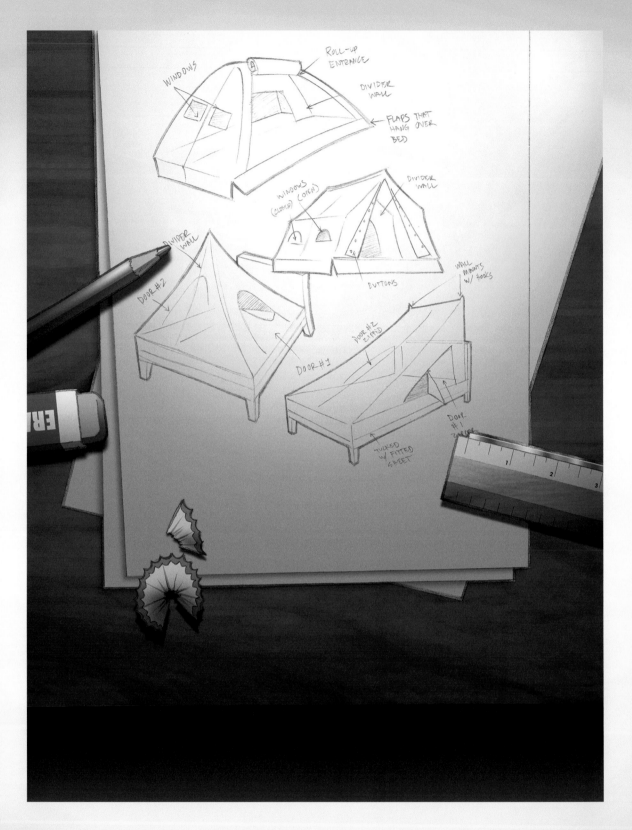

My mom helped me find a manufacturer, and for two years, I worked on four different prototypes before I developed my final product.

The Sleepover Bed Tent fits on a full or queen sized bed, and has a drop-down center panel that divides the bed in half to provide private sleeping spaces for two people.

Because there was not another product like mine on the market, my mother told me I should protect my idea by getting a patent on it. I learned that there are two different kinds of patents, utility patents that protect what a product does and design patents that protect what a product looks like. I met with my patent lawyer and he helped me file the patents for my invention, which is now patented as the "Slumber Separator".

There were several steps I needed to complete to start my business. I had to register my business with the state as a Limited Liability Corporation (LLC), secure a state sales tax certificate, get an Employer Identification Number (EIN) from the federal government, reserve a domain name for my website, design a logo, rent a mailbox, get a business phone, design a website, open a bank account and set up credit card processing to receive payments for my product.

To publicize my business, I had photographs taken and hired a videographer to film both promotional and instructional videos. We used the photos and videos to develop marketing materials. It sounds like a lot of work, and it is, but it is what you have to do to get a business started.

Finally, I launched my website, www.sleepoverbedtent.com, and had a huge party to celebrate the opening of the Sleepover Bed Tent Company. All of my friends attended the launch event for my new business. Everyone said they loved my product!

The enthusiasm for my product resulted in a lot of publicity. Several newspapers and television shows have interviewed me about how I came up with the idea, developed my product and began my journey as a teen entrepreneur.

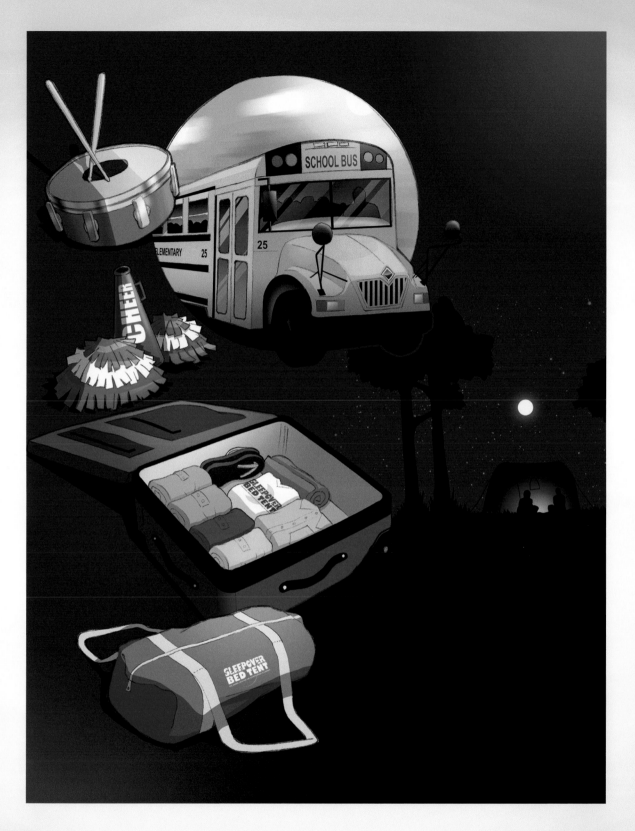

My tent is great for sleepovers, and because it comes in its own small carrying bag , it can also be used for school field trips, family vacations, sports team, cheerleader or band trips, church sleep-ins and even for camping when used on a blow up mattress.

I have had many opportunities to share my story of becoming a teen entrepreneur with other kids. I even went back to River Oaks Elementary school to encourage the students to participate in the Inventor's Showcase.

Many kids have great ideas and need to know that with hard work, they may be able to turn those ideas into the next big invention. I hope that my story will encourage other kids to turn their dreams into reality as kid entrepreneurs.

GLOSSARY OF TERMS

Entrepreneur: A person who starts a business enterprise and who is willing to take risks to make profits for that business.

Manufacturer: A person or company that owns a factory and makes goods for sale.

Prototype: A preliminary model of something.

Patent: A license from the government which gives a person or company the sole right to exclude others from making, using, or selling an invention.

Utility Patent: A patent that protects the way a product works.

Design Patent: A patent that protects the design or what a product looks like.

Limited Liability Corporation (LLC): A legal structure for a business which provides the limited liability benefits of a corporation but also allows for taxes to be paid by the partners.

Sales Tax Certificate: A document issued by the state to allow retailers to make taxable retail sales.

Employer Identification Number: A number assigned by the IRS to identify taxpayers who are required to file business tax returns.

Domain Name: A type of address that is used on the internet.

Website: A site or location on the internet that contains all of the information about your business.

Logo: A design adopted by a company to identify its product.

Credit Card Processing: Refers to a method for accepting payments by credit cards through the use of a company which charges a fee to process those payments.

Marketing Materials: Refers to all promotional or advertising materials used to promote a business or its products.

BUY THE SLEEPOVER BED TENT

The Sleepover Bed Tent is available online at www.sleepoverbedtent.com

Contact us: sales@sleepoverbedtent.com; Sleepover Bed Tent, LLC, 1302 Waugh Drive, #876, Houston, TX 77019.

Telephone: 713 320-6288

Like our Facebook Page: Sleepover Bed Tent

Follow us on Instagram: Sleepover_Bed_Tent

Printed in the United States
By Bookmasters